The Dogs of Humanity
By Colin Dardis

First published 2019 by Fly on the Wall Poetry Press

Published in the UK by
Fly on the Wall Poetry Press
56 High Lea Rd
New Mills
Derbyshire
SK22 3DP

www.flyonthewallpoetry.co.uk

ISBN: 978-1-9995986-9-3

The author acknowledges the kind support of the Arts Council of Northern
Ireland through their Artist Careers Enhancement Scheme, and the
Support for the Individual Artist Programme.

LOTTERY FUNDED

Thanks to...

God, for this blessing; my wife, Geraldine O'Kane for her constant belief and love; editor and publisher Isabelle Kenyon for her enthusiasm, professionalism, and general ability to be on top of everything(!); Damian Smyth and the Arts Council of Northern Ireland for their continual support and endorsement; you, for reading this.

Contents

One: Dogs

Raising the Bucket 6
The Dog at the Table 7
Mutton for the Mutt 8
People in Headphones 9
Bark, Ruff, Arf, Au Au, Bow-Wow, Yip 10
Stages 11
The Goalkeeper and the Postmistress 13
Ca-eight 14
Unpublished 15
Just 17
Catch 18
Yet Another Dog in an Otherwise Quiet Part of Town 19
Mad Dogs 20
You Want a Dog 21
The Wolf and its Howl 23
No More Legends 24
Runt 25

Two: Other Animals

Train Scenes 27
Elephant (Old Black Stars on Skies of Grey) 28
The Duck/Rabbit Effect 29
Fishing 30
Feline Comparison 31
Lion-Tree 32
Beachcombing 33
13 Ways of Looking at a Sparrow 34
Busy Blackbird 36
Blackbird of Belfast Lough 37
Farmyard 38
The Humane Animal 39

One: Dogs

Raising the Bucket

The presence of a well
at the garden's bottom
was enough to discourage
the cheekiest of birds,
their venture sports
confined to motorways
and cats.
         A dog once drowned
down there before you moved in,
you know, I remember the year.
After summer, and the longing of canines
was enough to encourage
a sad exploration.
If this tatterdemalion dog
was told in advance of his death,
he might have waited
until he knew what true thirst was.

The Dog at the Table

I am not moving towards you
in a way that is threatening
or foreboding. Trust me.

My steps are like my syntax,
measuring out in drops of caution,
spaced in order to give you breath.

As a girl might approach a boy
in a high street coffee shop
only after finishing her drink

might I come to you now
with a lip of foam hiding
the coquettishness of my walk.

And you will stay seated,
reading Milan Kundera's
The Book of Laughter

and Forgetting, as you get
lost in a sentence, and forget
to look up to the angels.

Look up from your borderline.
I'm tearing up the packets.
I'm adding sugar to your tea.

Mutton for the Mutt

I do not share your vernacular
or dine from the table of linguistics
you slob upon, crudely torn mutton
dangling from your mouth
with the gravy juice of language
smeared across butchering lips,
mopped up with a stale crust.

Feeling vegan
when presented with your meat,
unrecognisable joints and cutlets
gathered on the counter,
empathy with the blood.

People in Headphones

People in headphones
unaware of how their enthusiasm
is mistaken for idiocy,
shaking their heads like dogs eager for treats.
This is a sweet naivety on their part,
an attempt at privacy, unsuccessful;
their movements betraying seclusion
as public annoyance mounts.

Bark, Ruff, Arf, Au Au, Bow-Wow, Yip

I cannot come to you, little dog.
I cannot heal your barking with poison
or shut my ears no matter
how many doors and windows I close.

I am not your owner
or even a lover of dogs,
not wanting a kiss or a cuddle
in the way so many lonely people do.

All your words sound the same,
an angry repetition
born out of solitude and neglect.
I have cried the same tune,

spoken to the same dead air
and waited for the knock, the name,
the car engine, that familiar note
that only rings within the past.

Stages

Back then, you would go through the stages:
the voice box, the hair sprouts, the growth spurts;
now, you just stage passing *Go*
and pretend to hit all the required stations
while collecting your pay cheque at the end of the month.

And the thing about a Monopoly board
is that it's really a circle,
and the only way out
is either bankruptcy or jail.
Some of us get to land on Mayfair
or Park Avenue, but most sure can't afford
to stay there very long.
The rent collectors are out with their long knives
and the taxman is looking
to take everything you inherited:
from your father's shoelaces
to your mother's good graces and charm.

But I hid everything
in a deposit box somewhere,
left it to rust
and utilised nothing of my fortune;
that's why I'm such
a miserable wretch nowadays:
the dregs of the dogs,
down to his last stage.
There are no refunds, no guarantors,

and no one to underwrite your screw-ups.
God is coming to collect
and the riches He expects
won't be found in your pockets.

The Goalkeeper and the Postmistress
After Paul Durcan

He was a goalkeeper, and I am a postmistress
and every morning he would be there
at the other side of the door,
ready to catch the mail I slotted through.
His technique was faultless.

I tried arriving at different times;
stopped whistling so he wouldn't hear my approach;
ditched my postal-worker uniform
and came in plain clothes, and then in disguise,
my postbag hidden amidst the petunias.

He didn't even have a dog
to forebode my oncoming,
and still he was there, every time,
perfectly crouched, awaiting
the springtime of my ascent.
I never heard one of those letters
drop once onto his hallway
in all my years of delivery
and never found out
what was so damn important
inside all of his envelopes.

Ca-eight

The disproportionate dog
is mute with stiletto teeth
and feeds off hind legs
it carries in a teacup.

In the wooing season, his knees
cannot bend to bump, just
rub together as two matchsticks
alighting his oversized loins,
bollocks mirroring
the fires of Mars.

His cheeks cannot hold
the gallons of drool
that pool at his chops,
broken elastic lips failing to grip
onto waistbands of gum.

The poor mutt's spine
is almost a circle,
with a chest only covering
a few degrees,
but damn it if his tail
doesn't wag to my heartbeat,
always keeping up, always on the walk.

Unpublished

Life is a poor novelist:
it introduces too many characters
without explaining their role
and presupposes foreknowledge
on the part of the reader.

Askew, often, is syntax
in passages of persiflage,
highfalutin babble,
impenetrable even with
the best dictionary for translation.

The chapters dispense
with all sense of chronology
and hold insufficient answers:
subplots abandoned,
intrigue unsatisfied.

None of the pages are numbered,
no index for easy reference;
void of footnotes or appendix,
we are not granted the luxury
of books for further reading.

People walk about
with their dust jackets torn,
spines cracked, dog-eared
and yellowing, forgotten about
on the shelves of humanity.

Life would not reach print
by the high demands
of us human publishers,
yet it is the only manual
we have to read.

Just

What you imagined was a cat
lying bent at the side of a road?
It was just a buckled hubcap:
hush dear, and believe what you're told.

And that poor wee squish-squashed hedgehog?
Did you not see how it fluttered?
Just the wave of a paper bag
and *not* a pet that's been splattered.

That red furball? I know it looks
like the remains of some creature.
A curled-up dog? An urban fox?
That's just a discarded sweater.

Now silence there in the backseat,
settle down and go off to sleep.

Catch

If I was a dog,
you might be a stick,
and you'll throw yourself away
for me to try and catch you again.

If you were a dog
I would hope to be a stick,
with you wanting to run after me
and retrieve me again and again.

But we will end up as two sticks
with other dogs running after us;
you might be picked up
but I'll rather be left in the forest.

Yet Another Dog in an Otherwise
Quiet Part of Town

The yelping dog has been painted in
by a devilish town planner,
set to bark his unknown plight
through each turn of the hour.

Hades, guarding his own hell.

In my mind, all dogs are male,
the slobbering hair-soaked Cain
set to destruct. Or is he Able,
mourning his brother's turn?

He barks high and small,
a rubber ball hitting against glass,
deaf neglections and dead neighbours.
The soundtrack of our days,
the elasticity of youth.
Stamina.

Mad Dogs

Mad dogs, the lot of them
with only one bone to slobber over:
the bone of extradition,
proud difference,
practised segregation.

Standing cocksure
outside their kennel clubs and kennel houses,
sniffing for some foreign blood;
their world is a butcher shop's window
and you wonder how hungry
the dogs will be today.

Sweet flash of fang
and dropped snarls
bray in neighbouring airs,
a sniff of the fight;
then it's worthless to throw
your money into the ring:
no one wins here,
no one breaks from the leash.

You Want A Dog

You want a dog.

All the dogs of the world
want to lick the fingers
of a dutiful master,
the sweat of pork chops caught
under fingernails, sniffed at
by beautiful, wet snouts
of beast and man.

Beast and man come together
in the one bed, on the floor,
in the straw, the cold
straw of womanhood,
forgotten and broken
without a camel's back in sight.

You want a dog.

You want to take the lead
from off his neck
and place it on your own
You want to lie down in his bed
and claim it as your own.

You wish for someone to bring you
your meals in little doggy trays
and commence a simple diet.
You have no concern for walks,
just content to lie at home
in the fire-warmth
at the feet of your owner.
You would be obedient. Faithful.
All the splendid things
the character of a fine dog possesses.

You want a dog.
That dog is you.

The Wolf and its Howl

The wolf has been with us for a while now.

It watches us during love-making,
nibbles a corner of the bed sheet and drools on the linen.

It eats from our table, never waiting for mere scraps,
pleasing itself on the main meat.

It's the kick in our bellies when we cramp over from greed,
the silence of thoughts so loud,

providing a chisel to the nearest wall
to transcribe our lone bestial wails.

The wolf, it bleeds onto this rented household.
I do not know how it achieved its wounds.

Lupine mystery, we let it howl
without a moon to show its teeth.

We have no say in the lullaby.

No More Legends

Take Rapunzel down from her tower
to silence capriciousness;
bring Prometheus from off the crag
and give him bedding;
lead Llamrei and Hengroen from the waterside
and choke their spirit under hay.

All fathers crying, as they watch
their wolfhounds writhe from strychnine,
expected to be stoic and silent,
only conversing with the sword,
while Aisling tends the cows and hopes
the milk has not yet turned sour.

Our giants are now born
from laziness and prosperity,
without legend; their struggle,
to turn down collars, polish leather,
watch the daily news and continue feeding
while still savouring their bread.

Runt

The wind runs right through this cage.
When I raised my paws to the looped wire
a cold handshake greeted me. Now,
I dream of blankets, of others' fur.

When feeding time comes, I wait.
After, a hand arrives with a bottle
and I try to believe in the milk.
It's the mouth that lacks determination.

Across the way, the conversation
slips through the jostle. I have not been named,
so they never talk of me. I call myself *runt*,
a title earnt through exclusion.

Two: Other Animals

Train Scenes

Only the birds are out this morning.
The dogs remain crouched at their front doors,
fishermen choose the blanket over the reel.

The waves' flurry washes away
a scurry of sandpipers
as a train cuts through the mist.

It's a watercolour with grey wash
even the goats can't escape, the cows
anchored to their fields, stoic as rock.

Workmen abroad at Bellarina,
their hi-vis overalls two drops of sun
against this Autumn sky.

Underneath it all, a row of crows,
a tractor persisting,
a farm shed collapsing.

Elephant (Old Black Stars on Skies of Grey)

Your world dips down two narrow wells,
small space of primitive sense
allowing mortal dominance,
open pores on expansive swell.

Survey the sprawl, the jungle's breadth,
your kingdom tall; her hunters lie
to capture jewels beyond your eyes,
to quell the waters of your breath.

Who could stalk your bony fruit
while capturing that dark glint,
moistened wells, ring of flint?
Such agony of man's pursuit.

The Duck/Rabbit Effect
for Martelle McPartland

I am neither the duck, nor the rabbit,
or both slanted to some odd fusion,
not even held in one firm spot
for you to stare at my illusion.

The truth is some kind of paradox
in which I'm placed to at once
be the hope in Pandora's Box
and a woman of consequence.

Fishing

for Tom French

Took the sailboat out again today:
it's a distant shore now, getting further
and further away; shallower, even.
Still, once navigated, you can drop down,
deny the years' advancing winds
and just float. I have little say over
where the anchor plumbs: a lazy duck
on a canal's soft current, breaking at my back.

Some days, nothing bites and the sea is gone;
or, the fishing's good. I reel her in,
inspect the catch, judging weight, sense scales
slipping in my hands. I feel comfortable
in returning them to this ocean's shift.

Feline Comparison

Swoon of cloud erupts
in the only place fit:
above our sheltered world,
blessing brick and shale
for uniting in
such tidy composition.

Shed pity for the cat,
fur and night in unison;
sheen of slicker
flickering past street lamps,
incurious to nature,
a picture of stoicism.

Lion-Tree

A golden evening opening up before me
in the green pan of Lagan meadows;
one lazy pasture neatly circled
by two rivers,
                and held in their pan,
bowing down to the water,
this fallen oak: still a giant in death,
on his knees portraying humility.

Gone, the emperor cloth of leaves,
gone, the good wine-sap from earth;
now his naked roots hanging
as unabashed genitalia
warmed in the Solstice sun.

As the ass might approach
the elderly, ill lion,
I mounted him and proclaimed
myself king; with ginger footing,
reaching for the sun as a crown.

Beachcombing

Beachcombing, always the hope
of sighting ducks, their muddled wings
and goofy feet part of the charm.

And you, stuffed with innocence,
my invented thing, yet part of
my being, part of my home.

13 Ways of Looking at a Sparrow

1. If you challenge a sparrow directly, its friends will conspire to sully your washing line / car / jacket / whatever is most convenient.

2. Sparrows love to be told that they are handsome. Complimenting a sparrow on Midsummer's Day will bring you wealth.

3. Sparrows hate poetry. They do however like Archers fan fiction, written exclusively by middle-class retirees.

4. You must believe in the sparrow before you can see it.

5. The sparrow must believe in you before it allows you to see it.

6. Some sparrows are actually pigeons in disguise with identity crises.

7. Sparrows believe that photographs capture part of their soul and so have craftily learnt to avoid the lens.

8. Seeing a sparrow's shadow on April 13th is a sign of six more weeks of Spring.

9. Aspiring sparrows are often headhunted. Unfortunately, this is mostly always by sparrowhawks.

10. Holding the feather of a sparrow in your mouth while love-making is an ancient fertility rite.

11. The reason cats and sparrows don't get along dates back to the Great Class War of 1847.

12. Pigeons are secretly jealous of the sparrows' melliferous song. Sparrows in turn are openly jealous of starlings.

13. The collective noun for sparrows is a Franchised-Grocery-Store-At-Your-Local-Garage of sparrows.

Busy Blackbird

Bright bustle of beak
between bush,
bringing back blackberries.

Blackbird of Belfast Lough

translated from the 9th century Irish

Behold, some minor bird
giving out a loud yelp
from the tip of his
clear-yellow lip.

A blackbird
crafts his cry.
Belfast Lough
turns yellow.

Farmyard

There's a siren licking the air,
giving a pinch, a squeal;
a sheepdog roar
dividing the pack
and slicing mutton.

It's a farmyard out there,
with glamour cows
penned into the nightclubs,
lame lambs at the side of dance-floors
asking to be sacrificed.

Pigs swill from barrels and bottles;
the smell of the sty is high here.
While male equine beasts bray at barmen,
the females compete in dressage;
every night is a show jump.

There is no farmer
to round up the herds tonight.

The Humane Animal

How many are dying tonight?

How many tonight are listening
to make sure someone else is still breathing,
the dark seconds of void
where neither breath nor movement exist
and the other side of the bed
is the unconquerable distance
of a consciousness.

How many can't sleep tonight?
How many are unable to lay
despite their blackout curtains
drawn to the world,
the futility of fresh sheets
and lumbar support as useless
as an alarm clock for insomniacs.

How many are scared tonight?
How many want to burrow into the nest
like the newly-hatched cuckoo
and cry the loudest in order to be fed,
waiting to be recognised
as an imposter amongst the living
and thrown out of their present.

How many are unanswered tonight?

We all are. We all are. We all are.

Acknowledgements

Thank you to the editors of the following publications for originally printing some of these poems:
A New Ulster *(Unpublished)*
mgversion2>Datura *(Feline Comparison)*
Origami Poetry Project *(Train Scenes)*
Snapping Twig *(Runt)*
Stargazy Pie *(Catch)*
Visual Verse *(The Dog at the Table)*
wordlegs *(Dogs)*

Farmyard was commissioned as part of artist Brian Kielt's exhibition, 'Alternate State', Duncairn Arts Centre, Belfast, March 2015.

Blackbird of Belfast Lough was translated as part of the Arts Council of Northern Ireland funded project, The A to Z of Belfast.

The first line of *The Goalkeeper and His Postmistress* was taken from the poem 'The Rose of Blackpool' by Paul Durcan.

Author Biography

Colin Dardis is a poet, editor, and arts coordinator from Northern Ireland. He co-runs Poetry NI, a multimedia platform for poets.

Colin's work has been published widely throughout Ireland, the UK and USA. His poetry has been listed in the *Seamus Heaney Award for New Writing, Over The Edge New Writer of the Year Award*, and the *Dermot Healy International Poetry Competition*, amongst others.

Having had a speech impediment when younger, attending speech therapy classes throughout primary school, Colin's initial interest in language and words grew out of these formative experiences. His personal history of depression and mental illness is also an ongoing influence on his work, which has led to a number of poetry-related charity readings and work in this field.

He currently co-runs Poetry NI, a multi-media, multi-project platform for poetry, alongside his wife Geraldine O'Kane. In 2011, he co-founded the popular Purely Poetry monthly event in the Crescent Arts Centre, Belfast, building it up to become a cornerstone in the NI literary scene through open mics and poetry slams. In 2012, the first issue of FourXFour was released, an online quarterly poetry journal, showcasing new writing from Northern Ireland and beyond.

Previous collections include *the x of y* (Eyewear Publishing, 2018), *Post-Truth Blues* (Locofo Chaps/Moira Books, 2017) and *Dōji: A Blunder* (Lapwing Publications, 2013).

Author Website: www.colindardispoet.co.uk

About Fly on the Wall Press:

A publisher with a conscience.
Publishing high quality anthologies on pressing issues, chapbooks and poetry products, from exceptional poets around the globe.
Founded in 2018 by founding editor, Isabelle Kenyon.

Other publications:

Please Hear What I'm Not Saying (February 2018. Anthology, profits to Mind.)
Persona Non Grata (October 2018. Anthology, profits to Shelter and Crisis Aid UK.)
Bad Mommy/Stay Mommy by Elisabeth Horan (May 2019. Chapbook.)
The Woman With An Owl Tattoo by Anne Walsh Donnelly (May 2019. Chapbook.)
the sea refuses no river by Bethany Rivers (June 2019. Chapbook.)
White Light White Peak by Simon Corble (July 2019. Artist's Book.)
Second Life by Karl Tearney (July 2019. Full collection)

Social Media:

@fly_press (Twitter)
@flyonthewall_poetry (Instagram)
@flyonthewallpoetry (Facebook)
· flyonthewallpoetry.co.uk